D0615573

Latin for Pigs

Latin

An Illustrated History from

for Pigs

Oedipork Rex to Hog & Das

Lisa Angowski Rogak
and
Virginia Blackert

Illustrated by
Harry Trumbore

 A DUTTON BOOK

DUTTON
Published by the Penguin Group
Penguin Books USA Inc., 375 Hudson Street,
New York, New York 10014, U.S.A.
Penguin Books Ltd, 27 Wrights Lane, London W8 5TZ, England
Penguin Books Australia Ltd, Ringwood, Victoria, Australia
Penguin Books Canada Ltd, 10 Alcorn Avenue,
Toronto, Ontario, Canada M4V 3B2
Penguin Books (N.Z.) Ltd, 182–190 Wairau Road, Auckland 10, New Zealand

Penguin Books Ltd, Registered Offices:
Harmondsworth, Middlesex, England

First published by Dutton, an imprint of Dutton Signet,
a division of Penguin Books USA Inc.
Distributed in Canada by McClelland & Stewart Inc.

First Printing, November, 1994
10 9 8 7 6 5 4 3 2 1

Copyright © Lisa Angowski Rogak and Virginia R. Blackert, 1994

Illustrations Copyright © Harry Trumbore, 1994
All rights reserved

 REGISTERED TRADEMARK—MARCA REGISTRADA

LIBRARY OF CONGRESS CATALOGING-IN-PUBLICATION DATA
Rogak, Lisa Angowski.
    Latin for pigs : an illustrated history from Oedipork Rex to Hog
& Das / Lisa Angowski Rogak and Virgina Blackert ; illustrated by
Harry Trumbore.
      p.   cm.
    ISBN 0-525-93820-6
    1. Swine—Humor.   2. Latin—Humor.   3. Pig Latin—
Humor.   4. Puns
and punning.   I. Blackert, Virginia.   II. Trumbore, Harry.
III. Title.
PN6231.S895R64   1994
818'.5402—dc20   94-16666
                                                                             CIP

Printed in the United States of America
Set in Palatino
Designed by Eve L. Kirch

Without limiting the rights under copyright reserved above, no part of this
publication may be reproduced, stored in or introduced into a retrieval system,
or transmitted, in any form, or by any means (electronic, mechanical, photo-
copying, recording, or otherwise), without the prior written permission of both
the copyright owner and the above publisher of this book.

For Chris—L.R.

To my father, who always knew pigs were funny,
and to Arnie, who patiently kept
the hot water running—V.B.

For my piglets, Dale and Doug—H.T.

CONTENTS

INTRODUCTION

Ah, Latin for Pigs. Isn't that where you take the first letter of the word, stick it on the end, add an "ay" and . . .

Not anymore. Today, you don't have to warp your words in order to speak Latin for Pigs. All you need is a copy of this book and to look at the people and events of today—and yesterday—through sow-colored glasses.

For instance, who could have guessed that none other than Mikhail Boarbachev was really responsible for piggystroika. Too bad his human counterpart came along and claimed Boarbachev's successes as his own. Maybe if Boarbachev had prevailed, the USSR would still be cookin' up a storm.

Going back a couple of centuries, what about Narollypollean Bonaparte, one of France's greatest exports, besides pâté? Do you really want to know why the renowned French emperor is frequently shown posing with his hand in his shirt? Hint: remember the old saying that an army travels on its stomach. . . .

The literary figures of our time haven't escaped the influence of Latin for Pigs, either. From Harriet Beecher Sow, who penned the famous *Oinkle Tom's Cabin*, to the classic *Frankenswine*, Latin pigs have successfully carved out their place in history, as well as in our culture. When's the last time you heard the terms *Et tu, Porky* or *pigsonna non grata* and thought to give even a nod to the real source of these colorful phrases? Of course, it's none other than the founding fathers and mothers—or boars and sows—of Latin for Pigs.

Of course, the greatest thing about *Latin for Pigs* is that it's not just for pigs—it's for anyone who loves to wallow in porcine word play and is a glutton for piggy pun-ishment. So turn the page and test your stying—er—staying power. Soon you, too, may become fluent in Latin for Pigs.

1

Myths

OEDIPORK REX

The Greek dramatist Soph-hog-cles' tragic mytho-hog-gical hero provided us with a proto-type for the modern dysfunctional family. Cutting-edge research has linked the Oedipork Complex to a variety of eating disorders.

PIGMALION

Pigmalion was a prince of stately grease and beauty. But even after trying numerous dating services, Pigmalion could find no sow who met his exacting expectations for a mate. He decided to sculpt for himself a mate from tallow (pig fat, of course)—a perfect female to keep company with his perfect self. But when our self-righteous prince completed his statue and kissed its perfection, guess what? His breath brought her to life, she took one look at Pigmalion and decided that he was a pig after all, and she took off for greener pastures.

PORKASUS

Porkasus, twin brother of Pigasus, flew south rather than north into the sky. Penniless, he survived by performing aerial stunts at small-town carnivals and by foraging in the garbage cans behind the local Piggly-Wiggly.

ECHOG & NARCISSUI

Echog, a nymph, tried to win the heart of Narcissui, a conceited pig. When her love was not returned, Echog became so despondent that she faded away. She lost her final consonance and became a mere resonance of her former self, an echo. Meanwhile, Narcissui was so taken by his own reflection in a pond that he fell into the water and became a splash hit.

VENUS

Hogdess of love the world over and mother of Cupig (from the Latin *cuteus piggius*), Venus was known for her mi-sty-fying pigulcritude, and her talents in matchmaking made her the pick of the litter. Art lovers the world over have shelled out pig bucks for her porktrait.

HAMALANTA & HIPHOGMENES

Many boars wanted to marry the beautiful but independent Princess Hamalanta. She answered each with a challenge: He could race her, but if he lost, he would be butchered. "If you win," said Hamalanta, "I will marry you." Needless to say, many young princes ended up on the wrong end of a spit due to Hamalanta's hurrying hamstrings.

One young boar, Hiphogmenes, appealed to Venus to help him win Hamalanta's heart. Venus gave Hiphogmenes three golden apples. Then Hiphogmenes challenged Hamalanta to race. During the race, Hiphogmenes tossed the golden apples one at a time off to the side. Hamalanta chased after each apple, which slowed her down and enabled Hiphogmenes to win the race. But when she found out Hiphogmenes had tricked her and had no more apples, she had him served at the royal barbecue. Later, she settled down with a boar who was long in the tusk but who owned a large orchard.

2

The
Arts
and

Sciences

PIGGELANGELO

The Italian-born artist, sculptor, painter, architect, and poet created the frescoes on the ceiling of the Pigstine (sometimes known as the Cistern) Chapel. With his eyes toward the heavens, the supine swine lay down in pigstory as a genius of the Penaissance.

HARRIET BEECHER SOW

This nineteenth-century antislavery author wrote the controversial classic *Oinkle Tom's Cabin*.

CHARLIE "YARDBIRD" PORKER

This jazz great had an ear for the alto sax and, along with Dizzy Gillespig, sired bebop. Porker needed no prodding to stray from the beaten path and produce a bumper harvest of sound.

GIACOMO PIGCCINI

La Boarheme is one of the best-loved triumphs of Pigccini, who remains known for his endings in which the fat lady sings.

PIGNIC IN THE GRASS

Claude Monet, a French painter of the 1800s, believed in pigs' primary theory, a physical enjoyment of life. This phil-hog-sophy was the basis for his painting, the lovely and pastoral *Pignic in the Grass*, which shocked the world by showing a female model wearing nothing but her pigskin.

SWINE LAKE

Aspiring ballerinas throughout the world have coveted the role of Swineddette, the lovely swan princess, in composer Tchaich-hog-sky's *Swine Lake*. In the composer's original version, the swine and her mortal lover sank to the bottom of a mud puddle, becoming nothing more than soggy pork chops. In a subsequent version performed more than twenty years later, however, assistant ballet master Lev Hogganov added a spectacular ending, with the lovers and the entire pork de ballet frolicking in hog heaven.

PABLO PIGCASSO

This leader in the field of modern art decided to depart from everybody else's idea of painting and pig out. His Blue Period and Rose Period were followed by his lesser-known Pork Period, which de-pig-ted lifestyles of the common swine. He began the cubist movement, a style that broke all subjects down into platter-size components.

BOARISHNIKOV

His greaseful leaps and sty-lish elegance have made this Russian-bred dancer the creme of the corps. After each performance he soaks his hooves in a briny solution—hence the expression "pickled pigs' feet."

HOGGY CARMICHAEL

A jazz musician of the 1920s, he composed songs such as "Stydust" and "Hoggy River," that became favorites of artists Louis Hamstring and Benny Goodpig.

LEONARD BERNSWINE

As the musical director and conductor of the New York Phil-hog-monic orchestra, he composed not only classical masterpieces but also such Broadway classics as *Canned Pig* and *West Side Deli*.

PIGGAROTTI

The world's most beloved tenor has been sus-
pected of fitting in a meal or two between arias.
He consistently drives audiences to squeals with
his tasty servings of "Prosciutto Non Troppo"
and other love songs.

MICKEY POURKE

American sex-symbol film actor. His many fighting, drooling, and grunting roles in films such as *Barpig* and *9½ Squeals* won the hearts of French cinema goers.

MICKEY POURKE
IN THE PIG OF
GREENWICH VILLAGE

LE FESTIVAL
DU FILM
AVEC

JERRY
LEWIS
ET
MICKEY
POURKE

AL PIGCINO

We've all had those days . . . and the talent of superstar Al Pigcino immortalized the tail of a street-tough little piggy who refused to cry "wee, wee, wee" all the way home.

PYGTHAGORAS

This sixth-century Greek phil-hog-sopher and mathematician founded a religious society in Italy that practiced vegetarianism. His sloppy eating habits left him hungry, or at least unsatisfied, most of the time and led to the accomplishment for which he is most remembered—the theory of the pyg-thagorean triangle, which was nothing more than the path of his ritual march from bed to refrigerator to table.

HIPPORKRATES

This historic curer of hams originated the Hip-porkcratic oath, which guides the medical profession in its attempts to balance between the frying pan and the fire. The original oath has been amended in recent years to include the swine-boggling privileges now considered an ap-pen-dage to most medical careers.

ALBERT EINSWINE

With his theory of relativity, Einswine revolutionized modern physics, which sought to answer the age-old question "Why does time stand still when you're waiting for dinner to be served?" His formula $E=MC_2$ showed hungry scientists that Eating is twice as good as Math Class.

MARIE CURIE

This French scientist invented a quick-smoke way to curie hams and bacon as a side step on her journey to an alimentary new discovery.

3

Leaders

HAMMIBLE

The pignacious general led a squad of elephants over the Alps and took the Romans—midbarbecue—by surprise.

LORD JEFFREY HAMERST

This British general served in the American col-
onies just prior to 1776. Finding the colonists re-
volting, he went back to England, but Hamerst
College in western Massachusetts was neverthe-
less named for him. Students at the prestigious
college often scoff at those mispronouncing *Am-
herst* by sounding the *h* in the second syllable,
though it actually belongs at the beginning of
the name. A movement is a-hoof to change the
name of a local river to Rye.

PIGGAHONTAS

Indian daughter of Pighatan, chief of the Pighatan confederacy of Virginia. Without her,
John Smith would have become the first Virginia ham.

NAROLLYPOLLEAN BONAPARTE

Great military hero of France, he conquered half the world and its tables and crowned himself emperor of France in 1804. In pictures, he's generally depicted thrusting his hand into his shirt, most likely to reach for a snack.

THE YALTA(ED) MILK &
A SLICE OF THE WORLD
CONFERENCE

Allied leaders Hoggston Churchill, Franklin Delano Roose-svelt, and Jowlseph Stylin planned the final course of World War II at a table in Yalta on February 4–11, 1945. Known as the "Pig Three," they divided up the world like pigs at a trough, but they didn't realize they were biting off more than they could chew.

SWINE AND EVITA PIGRONE

The first couple of Argentina during the 1940s, this piggy pair came to power on the strength of their loyal *descamisados*, who cared more for bacon than proper dress. The Pigrones, and Evita in particular, raised hog-nobbing with royalty and living high on the hog to a fine art.

HOG CHI MINH

Although rather thin for a member of the porcine family, he led his countrymen to a Viet Hog victory.

MIKHAIL BOARBACHEV

His policy of piggystroika opened up Russia to all the delicious excesses of the West. Russians quickly showed their appetite for American sneakers, jeans, and Big Macs.

SADHAM HOGSAIN

Everybody's favorite villain, this little piggy invaded Kuwait, an act of overindulgence that led to the Engulf War. American Pigtroit missiles soon had him on the run with his tail between his legs.

4

Legends

HAMLET, PRINCE OF DENMARK

With his brother, Omelette, and cousin Cutlet, Hamlet posed the universal question, "To eat or not to eat?" Ghostly goings-on in the castle drove them to the kitchen where, for a little recreation, they invented the Danish pastry.

LIZZIE BOARDEN

Slaughtering time at the old Boarden farm! Little Lizzie wasn't about to become suckling pig, though; she beat them all to it with her trusty ax and cut out of there, leaving 250 pounds of pork chops behind.

FRANKENSWINE

Perhaps the most feared pig in all literature, this fantastic monster was a pigment of Mary Shelley's imagination. He tormented and ultimately destroyed his own creator, probably because of a disagreement over diet.

ROBIN HOG

In the days of King Arthur (ruler of the kingdom of flour and lard) the dashing outlaw Robin Hog roamed the English countryside in search of injustice. With his lovely mistress Maid Maryoink and his merry band of knights in shining pigskin, he robbed the rich of great stores of pork chops, bacon, and gravy and gave them to the poor. Robin was captured when the arist-hog-racy began to feel deprived of their daily rasher of bacon with fried eggs at high tea due to the dearth of pork Robin was producing in the market.

HOG & DAS

Forerunners of Ben & Jerry, the ice cream boys from Vermont, Hog & Das are far too shy to plaster their pigtures on the cartons of their rich, creamy confections. These two are, however, giving just desserts to millions of overfed but smilingly contented Americans.

5

Language
Legacies

ET TU, PORKY
"Thanks a lot, pal."

PIGSONNA NON GRATA
". . . and stay out!"

ERRARE SWINANUM
"To err is piggish."

66

HABEAS PORCUS
"You must have a pig."

IN VINO VERITAS
"In swine the truth."

COGITO, ERGO SUM PORCUS
"I think, therefore I am a pig."

PORCUS IN HORTO DORMIT
"Let sleeping pigs lie."

CAVE PORCUM
"Beware of the pig."

CAVEAT EMPTOR
"Sellers can be real pigs."

DE GUSTIBUS NON EST DISPUTANDUM
"One person's pig-out is another person's slops."

QUI ME AMAT, AMAT ET PORCUM MEUM
"Love me, love my pig."

TERES ATQUE ROTUNDUS
"A pig should be well rounded."

VESTIS PORCUM FACIT
"Clothing makes the pig."

PORCI CUM MARGARITAS
"Swine with Drinks."

6

Elements

of

Latin

for

Pigs

ROMAN NUMERALS

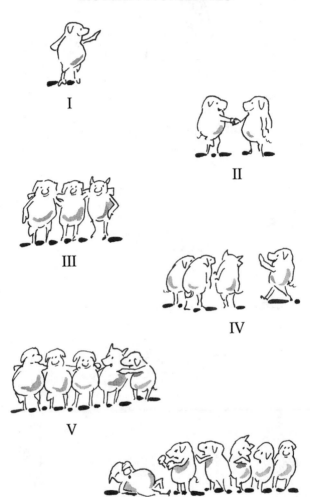

I

II

III

IV

V

VI

VII

VIII

IX

X

XI

XII

VOCABULARY

PUER
(N., masc.) - boy

PUELLA
(N., fem.) - girl

AGRICOLA
(N., masc.) - farmer

VERBS

AMO - V.,
first person singular
present tense
"I love"

AMAS - V.,
second person singular
present tense
"you love"

AMAT - V.,
third person singular
present tense
"he, she, or it loves"

SENTENCE STRUCTURE

"GALLIA EST OMNIS
DIVISA IN PARTES TRES"
("All Gaul is divided into three parts")
—Julius Caesar

"JACTA ALEA EST"
("The die is cast.")

—Julius Caesar

"VENI, VIDI, VINCI"
("I came, I saw, I conquered.")
—Julius Caesar